COLLEGE GOATs

THE GREATEST OF ALL TIME

GOATs OF COLLEGE HOCKEY

BY CHARLIE BEATTIE

SportsZone

An Imprint of Abdo Publishing

abdobooks.com

abdobooks.com

Published by Abdo Publishing, a division of ABDO, PO Box 398166, Minneapolis, Minnesota 55439.

Printed in the United States of America, North Mankato, Minnesota.
102025
012026

Cover Photo: Richard T. Gagnon/Getty Images Sport/Getty Images
Interior Photos: Jack Riddle/Denver Post/Getty Images, 5; Steve Powell/Getty Images Sport/Getty Images, 6; University of Minnesota, 9; David Madison/Getty Images Sport/Getty Images, 10; North Dakota Athletics, 13; Monte Rand/Bruce Bennett/Getty Images, 14; Al Behrman/AP Images, 17; Damian Strohmeyer/Sports Illustrated/Getty Images, 18; Steve Burmeister/AP Images, 21; David E. Klutho/Sports Illustrated/Getty Images, 22; Stew Milne/AP Images, 25; Elsa/Getty Images Sport/Getty Images, 26, 29, 30; Carlos Gonzalez/NCAA Photos/Getty Images, 32–33; Richard T. Gagnon/Getty Images Sport/Getty Images, 34, 38; Matt Marriott/NCAA Photos/Getty Images, 36–37; Stacy Bengs/AP Images, 40–41; Justin Berl/NCAA Photos/Getty Images, 42

Editor: Dalton Rains
Series Designer: Kate Liestman

Library of Congress Control Number: 2025939140

Publisher's Cataloging-in-Publication Data

Names: Beattie, Charlie, author.
Title: GOATs of college hockey / by Charlie Beattie
Description: Minneapolis, Minnesota: Abdo Publishing, 2026 | Series: College GOATs: the greatest of all time | Includes online resources and index.
Identifiers: ISBN 9781098298326 (lib. bdg.) | ISBN 9798384932123 (ebook)
Subjects: LCSH: College sports--Juvenile literature. | Hockey--Juvenile literature. | Winter sports--Juvenile literature. | Sports records--Juvenile literature. | College sports--Records--Juvenile literature.
Classification: DDC 796.96263--dc23

TABLE OF CONTENTS

KEITH MAGNUSON

When Keith Magnuson arrived at Denver in 1965, freshmen weren't allowed to play varsity sports. The 6-foot, 185-pound defenseman hit the ice with the Pioneers' top team in 1966–67. His gritty, hard-hitting play quickly made him a menace during games. After the season, he was named co–Sophomore of the Year in the Western Collegiate Hockey Association (WCHA).

As great as Magnuson played in games, his hard work and determination also set a high standard in practice. Magnuson constantly pushed teammates to work as hard as he did. Despite that intensity, he was a beloved teammate. He was known as a hard-edged player on the ice but incredibly kind away from the rink.

The hard work and chemistry paid off for Magnuson and the Pioneers in 1967–68. Anchoring Denver's physical defense, he helped the Pioneers reach the 1968 National Collegiate Athletic Association (NCAA) championship game. Magnuson aggressively defended the goal while forcing turnovers all over the ice. That defensive effort helped Denver trounce North Dakota 4–0 for the program's fourth title.

FAST FACT

Magnuson went on to play for the Chicago Blackhawks. He made two National Hockey League (NHL) All-Star teams. He later coached for the Blackhawks.

Magnuson was named team captain as a senior in 1968–69. He continued to shine on defense. And he also posted 34 points in 32 games. The Pioneers returned to the national championship game. Denver broke a 2–2 tie early in the third period. Magnuson's standout defense helped the Pioneers hold on for a 4–3 win and a second straight title. His legacy lived on for decades. Nearly 40 years later, Denver's longtime coach George Gwozdecky was asked about the former standout. He called Magnuson "Mr. Pioneer."

Keith Magnuson, *left*, was a two-time All-American with Denver.

MARK JOHNSON

Mark Johnson arrived at the University of Wisconsin in 1977. By then, his father was already a legend at the school. Known as "Badger Bob," Robert Johnson had been coaching the Badgers' men's hockey team since 1964. He led the team to a national

Mark Johnson, *left*, celebrates a goal in the 1980 Olympic Games.

championship in 1973. However, it didn't take long for the younger Johnson to make a name for himself too.

By then, freshmen had become eligible to play on varsity teams. But no first-year player had taken over the college hockey world quite like Johnson did. The 5-foot-9 center tallied 36 goals and 44 assists in 43 games. At the time, his 80 points were an NCAA record for freshmen. More importantly, Wisconsin's father-son duo led the Badgers to the national championship game. Johnson recorded two goals and an assist in a 6–5 overtime win over Michigan.

A skilled shooter with a knack for big goals, Johnson played two more seasons at Wisconsin. He finished his college career with a program-record 125 goals in 125 games. In total, he posted 256 career points. More than 40 years later, that remained the second-most in Badgers history.

Johnson played in the NHL from 1980 to 1990. After that, he followed in his father's footsteps and became a coach. In 2002, he took over the Badgers' women's hockey team. Johnson built the program into a dynasty. In 2025, he won his eighth title as head coach.

FAST FACT

Johnson competed in the 1976 Olympic Games while still in high school. Four years later, he was the United States' leading scorer at the 1980 Olympics. Johnson scored twice in the famous "Miracle on Ice" upset against the Soviet Union. Days later, Team USA won a gold medal.

NEAL BROTEN

Neal Broten scored 21 goals as a freshman at Minnesota in 1978–79. But it was the forward's final goal of the season that became college hockey lore. The shot cemented the Roseau, Minnesota, native as a legend in his home state.

The Golden Gophers led North Dakota 3–2 in the third period of the 1979 national championship game. Broten carried the puck into the North Dakota zone. But he lost control as he tried to deke around a defender. Even then, Broten didn't give up on the play. Still slipping around, he lunged to reach the puck. He managed to whip a shot past North Dakota goalie Bob Iwabuchi. Broten's spectacular effort proved to be the game-winning goal in a 4–3 victory.

Broten left the Gophers after that season to train with the US Olympic team. After winning a gold medal at the 1980 Games in Lake Placid, New York, he returned to Minnesota for one more season. It was as if he'd never left. Broten put up 17 goals and 54 assists in just 36 games. Many of his assists went to his younger brother, Aaron,

FAST FACT

The Hobey Baker Award was named for a player who starred in hockey and football at Princeton in the early 1910s. His exact hockey stats are unknown. However, it is estimated that Baker piled up more than 100 goals and 100 assists in his career.

who led the team with 47 goals. After the season, the elder Broten was the first recipient of the Hobey Baker Award. Since 1981, the trophy has gone to the best men's player in college hockey.

Neal Broten set a Minnesota freshman record with 50 assists in 1978–79.

MARK FUSCO

At 5-foot-9 and 175 pounds, Mark Fusco was undersized for a defenseman. Even so, he more than held his own in the Harvard defensive zone during the early 1980s. But Fusco did his best work at the other end of the ice.

Former Harvard defenseman Mark Fusco, *center*, competed at the 1984 Olympic Games.

The Massachusetts native's swift skating kept defenders on edge during his four years with the Crimson. Fusco put up a combined 49 points in his first two seasons. As a junior in 1981–82, he set a team record for defensemen with 40 points. He broke the record again as a senior. This time he scored 13 goals and added 33 assists. His 46 points were a Crimson record for defensive players until Adam Fox topped the mark in 2018–19.

Fusco's play elevated Harvard to new heights as well. The Crimson posted losing records in his first three seasons. Then, as a senior, Fusco led Harvard to the 1983 NCAA Tournament. Few expected the Crimson to make a deep run. Instead, they upset Minnesota in the semifinals to clinch Harvard's first national championship game appearance.

Fusco's play earned him numerous awards. He was named to the All-East Coast Athletic Conference (ECAC) team in all four of his seasons. He was also a three-time All-American. Fusco capped his memorable career by winning the Hobey Baker Award in 1983. The award was in just its third year at the time, and Fusco was the first defenseman to win it.

FAST FACT

Three years after Mark Fusco won the Hobey Baker Award, his younger brother, Scott, took home the trophy. A star forward for the Crimson, Scott scored 24 goals and added 44 assists during the 1985–86 season. The Fuscos are still the only pair of brothers to have won the award.

TONY HRKAC

Tony Hrkac had a solid freshman year at North Dakota. The 5-foot-10, 170-pound forward posted 18 goals and 36 assists during the 1984–85 season. After that, the Thunder Bay, Ontario, native left to train with Canada's Olympic team. He returned to college for the 1986–87 season. That's when he really became a legend.

Hrkac was a blur on the ice. The sophomore helped North Dakota open the season with eight straight wins. In those games, the team's fast-paced offense outscored opponents a combined 58–24. As North Dakota blew out each new opponent, the media dubbed the team "The Hrkac Circus."

By the end of the season, Hrkac had racked up an NCAA-record 116 points. He was just as dominant in the postseason as he was in the regular season. Hrkac scored four points in the NCAA Tournament semifinals to lift North Dakota to the national championship game. The team then capped off the season with a 5–3 win over Michigan State. Hrkac didn't tally a point in the title game. But he was still named the tournament's Most Outstanding Player (MOP).

Hrkac also became the first North Dakota player to win the Hobey Baker Award. The sophomore left for the NHL after that season. But his dominant year left a lasting impact on the sport. As college hockey scoring has gone down since the 1980s, many experts think the forward's single-season scoring record will never be topped.

North Dakota forward Tony Hrkac averaged 2.46 points per game in 1986–87.

PAUL KARIYA

Players like Paul Kariya usually didn't play college hockey. The 5-foot-10 winger was a star growing up in British Columbia. Most figured he'd go on to a Canadian junior league before moving on to

In 1994, Maine winger Paul Kariya became the first freshman to win the Hobey Baker Award.

the NHL. Instead, Kariya was drawn to Maine. The school had built a successful program over the years.

The skinny 17-year-old freshman arrived for the 1992–93 season. Right away, he showed off his blazing-fast skating. He also always seemed to know where everyone was on the ice. He often stayed one step ahead of opponents. Kariya and senior captain Jim Montgomery led Maine to a 30–0–1 record to start the 1992–93 season. The Black Bears then fought their way through the NCAA Tournament. A 4–3 overtime win over Michigan lifted them to the title game.

Maine faced defending champion Lake Superior State in the national championship. Four minutes into the third period, the Black Bears trailed 4–2. Then Kariya escaped a defender behind the goal. He sent a pass to Montgomery, who slapped in a score to cut the lead down to one. A few minutes later, Kariya assisted on another Montgomery goal.

Soon after the game-tying score, a Lake Superior State penalty put Maine into a power play. Before long, Kariya was flying toward the net again. He received a pass from Montgomery, then sent the puck right back. Montgomery scored to give Maine a lead.

In less than five minutes, the freshman Kariya had assisted on three Montgomery goals. Maine held on for the 5–4 victory. The assists gave Kariya a nation-leading 100 points for the season. In the three decades since, no men's college player tallied that much.

Kariya's college career proved short. He piled up eight goals and 16 assists in the first 12 games of the 1994–95 season. After that, he left school to compete for Canada in the Olympic Games. But his legendary freshman season had taken its place in hockey lore.

BRENDAN MORRISON

Michigan center Brendan Morrison sped toward the goal. A teammate took a shot. But Colorado College's goalie deflected it. Morrison pounced on the rebound and slapped in a score. The goal broke a 2–2 tie in overtime of the 1996 national championship game. The Wolverines' bench cleared as teammates swarmed Morrison.

The win marked the peak of a dramatic rise for Michigan. The Wolverines hadn't won a national title for three decades. But Morrison's arrival in 1993–94 sparked a new era. The young Canadian immediately showed his talent. The Central Collegiate Hockey Association (CCHA) named him Rookie of the Year. The next season, Morrison earned his second straight All-Conference honor.

Heading into the 1996 title game, the junior Morrison had already posted a career-high 27 goals. His game-winner was number 28. The finish captured what made Morrison such a clutch player. He always knew what to do around the net. When it came time to score, the 5-foot-11, 180-pound star was often in the perfect position.

FAST FACT

Scores in college hockey were much higher in the 1970s and 1980s than they are today. As of 2025, 19 of the sport's 20 highest scorers played at least one season in those two decades. Morrison was the only exception. His 284 career points ranked 11th all-time.

Morrison came back to Michigan for his senior season in 1996–97. He made more school history. After finishing the year with 31 goals and 57 assists, Morrison won the Hobey Baker Award. He was the first Wolverine to take home the trophy.

Brendan Morrison (9) celebrates after his game-winning goal in the 1996 national championship game.

CHRIS DRURY

Chris Drury had always been a winner. At 12 years old, the Connecticut native played in the 1989 Little League World Series. Drury pitched in his team's championship game victory. Years later, he led his high school to a state championship in hockey.

Chris Drury (18) averaged 1.4 points per game with Boston University.

In 1995, Drury brought his winning mindset to Boston University. The Terriers had reached the national championship game in the previous season. But they'd fallen to Lake Superior State in a 9–1 rout. The freshman tallied 27 points in 39 games on the way to the 1996 national title game. Drury played on the fourth line in a 6–2 win over Maine.

The 5-foot-10 center continued moving up in the Terriers' lineup after that. And Boston University continued to pile up big wins. The Terriers won four straight Hockey East titles. They also won the Beanpot Trophy each season. The Beanpot is a yearly tournament between the four major college hockey teams in the Boston area.

Drury continued to rack up individual accolades as well. By his senior season in 1997–98, he had become a scoring star. He finished his career with a school-record 113 goals. All that scoring helped him earn Hockey East Player of the Year honors twice. As a senior, he also became Boston University's first Hobey Baker Award winner.

However, it was Drury's leadership that most impressed his teammates. As a junior, he was an alternate captain for the Terriers. He was co-captain alongside defenseman Sean Kelleher as a senior. In an early season interview, the defenseman said everyone on the team, including Kelleher himself, looked up to Drury. After college, Drury had a long career in the NHL, but he never outgrew his legendary status in Boston.

JENNIFER BOTTERILL

The first college women's hockey teams formed in the 1960s. Yet the NCAA still hadn't recognized the women's game when Jennifer Botterill arrived at Harvard in 1998. That meant the school didn't have a varsity team.

Botterill shone on the school's club team instead. The playmaking center from Winnipeg, Manitoba, was a great skater. Her supreme balance helped her stay in control on the ice. She used her powerful skating to stay ahead of opponents and her playmaking abilities to set up teammates. Over two seasons, she piled up 150 points in 51 games.

The NCAA finally started recognizing women's hockey in 2000–01. Botterill was ready. She posted 42 goals and 78 points in 30 games. After the season, she won the Patty Kazmaier Award as the top player in women's hockey.

Botterill took off the next college season to compete with Canada at the 2002 Olympic Games in Salt Lake City, Utah. She was back to smashing records at Harvard for the 2002–03 season.

FAST FACT

Like Hobey Baker decades before her, Patty Kazmaier was an accomplished athlete at Princeton University. Kazmaier excelled on the ice between 1981 and 1986. She died of a rare blood disease in 1990. Eight years later, the Patty Kazmaier Award was named in her honor.

On January 28, 2003, Botterill recorded 10 points against Boston College. In the following two decades, only one other college player matched that single-game mark. Botterill's seven assists that game also tied an NCAA record that she had set earlier in the season.

Botterill finished her senior season with an NCAA-record 112 points in 32 games. Minnesota's Natalie Darwitz broke that record when she scored 114 in 2004–05. However, Darwitz did so while playing eight more games than Botterill. Botterill's legacy lives on in other ways. In 2003, she won her second Kazmaier Award. As of 2025, she was still the only two-time winner.

Harvard center Jennifer Botterill, *left*, scored 157 career goals.

RYAN MILLER

Ryan Miller was born in East Lansing, Michigan, home of Michigan State. Three of his older cousins had been star forwards on the Spartans' men's hockey team in the 1980s and 1990s.

Michigan State goalie Ryan Miller was an NCAA West first-team All-American in 2001 and 2002.

When Miller joined the team in 1999, he immediately began adding to the family's legacy.

A 6-foot-2, 160-pound goalie, Miller read the game well and never seemed to get fazed. This helped him post a 16–5–3 record with eight shutouts as a freshman. His 1.53 goals-against average and .932 save percentage set school records. One opposing coach said the only way to score on Miller was to hope he gave up a rebound.

As a sophomore, Miller won 31 of his 40 games. He set NCAA records by stopping 95 percent of the shots he faced and shutting out opponents 10 times. Miller allowed only 1.32 goals per game while lifting the Spartans to an appearance in the Frozen Four. It's rare for a goalie to win the Hobey Baker Award, but the choice was easy in 2001. Miller became the first goalie to win the award since 1988.

Miller spent one more season in net for Michigan State. He added eight more shutouts in 2001–02, bringing his career total to 26. That number was still a record more than two decades after Miller's college career ended.

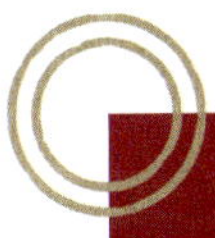

FAST FACT

Miller's cousins were all excellent offensive players at Michigan State. Kelly Miller posted 164 points in 165 games from 1981 to 1985. Kevin Miller tallied 201 points in 143 games from 1984 to 1988. The youngest brother, Kip Miller, finished his career with 261 points in 176 games from 1986 to 1990. Kip won the Hobey Baker Award as a senior.

KRISSY WENDELL

Dartmouth took an early 1–0 lead over Minnesota in the semifinals of the 2004 women's NCAA Tournament. That's when sophomore Krissy Wendell took over. The Minnesota forward scored a game-tying goal in the second period. Then, 7:29 into the third period, she slapped in her second goal of the night. A few minutes later, Wendell scored for the third time. The unassisted goal gave her a hat trick. It also gave the Golden Gophers a commanding 4–1 lead. Wendell later posted an assist to put the finishing touches on the 5–1 victory.

Wendell's hat trick lifted Minnesota to the national championship game. In that game, she tallied a goal and three assists in a 6–2 win over Harvard. With eight points in two games, the forward established a new Frozen Four record.

Wendell came to the Gophers from nearby Brooklyn Park, Minnesota. The hometown star made a habit of piling up goals and assists. After tallying 55 points as a freshman in 2002–03, Wendell posted 78 as a sophomore. Opponents even had to keep an eye on her when Minnesota was shorthanded. As a junior

FAST FACT

Krissy Wendell teamed up with fellow legend Natalie Darwitz at Minnesota. Darwitz, a 5-foot-3 forward, set the NCAA single-season scoring record. She posted 114 points in 2004–05.

in 2004–05, Wendell used her quick hands and blazing speed to post an NCAA record of seven shorthanded goals. She finished that season with 104 points and became the first Minnesota player to win the Kazmaier Award.

The Gophers returned to the Frozen Four in 2005. This time, Wendell had two goals and two assists in a 7–2 win over Dartmouth in the semifinals. She then opened the scoring in the final against Harvard and later assisted on the Gophers' third goal. Minnesota won 4–3.

Forward Krissy Wendell, *left*, averaged 2.35 points per game during her time with Minnesota.

Wisconsin goalie Jessie Vetter, *center*, was the Frozen Four MOP in both 2006 and 2009.

JESSIE VETTER

Three hockey dynasties ruled the first decade of women's NCAA hockey. The Minnesota-Duluth Bulldogs won each year from 2001 to 2003. The Minnesota Gophers then took home back-to-back titles in 2004 and 2005. In 2006, Wisconsin was poised to begin its own dynasty. The Badgers owed much of their success to standout goalie Jessie Vetter.

Vetter grew up just outside of Madison, Wisconsin, where the Badgers' campus is located. In 2006, the hometown star led the team to the Frozen Four. The Badgers shut out St. Lawrence 1–0 in the semifinals. It was the first-ever shutout by a women's goalie in the Frozen Four. Two days later, the freshman posted the second shutout. She blanked Minnesota 3–0 and won the tournament's MOP Award.

Vetter led the Badgers back to the NCAA Tournament in 2007. In the opening round, the sophomore held off Harvard through four overtime periods before Wisconsin finally came through with a 1–0 victory. By the time Vetter once again blanked St. Lawrence in the semifinals, she had run her NCAA Tournament–shutout streak to 508 minutes and five seconds. Minnesota-Duluth finally scored on Vetter in the championship game. Not that it mattered. Wisconsin still won 4–1.

The Badgers reached the title game again in 2008, but they fell to Minnesota-Duluth. Vetter continued dominating the next season. She allowed only 1.26 goals per game as a senior. In the Frozen Four, she stopped 65 out of 66 shots. She posted her fourth career Frozen Four shutout in a 5–0 victory over Mercyhurst in the title game.

MEGHAN AGOSTA

As a teenager, forward Meghan Agosta helped Canada win gold at the 2006 Olympics in Turin, Italy. Any college team would have loved to have her. However, in a surprise to many fans, Agosta decided to attend Mercyhurst in Erie, Pennsylvania. The Lakers had been a strong team in the smaller College Hockey America conference. But they had never won an NCAA Tournament game.

Mercyhurst had also never had a scorer like Agosta. Using her great speed, soft hands, and accurate shots, the 5-foot-6 freshman poured in 38 goals in 2006–07. That helped her become the first freshman finalist for the Patty Kazmaier Award. She was only getting started.

With Agosta leading the way, Mercyhurst reached new levels of success. In 2008–09, the junior helped the Lakers earn the nation's No. 1 ranking for the first time. During one stretch, Agosta tallied four hat tricks in a row. She totaled 14 goals and three assists through the red-hot four-game streak.

FAST FACT

Agosta took a year away from Mercyhurst to compete in the 2010 Olympic Games. She was the top scorer of the Games and was voted Most Valuable Player as she led Canada to a gold medal. Agosta added another gold medal in 2014 and a silver in 2018.

Mercyhurst opened that year's NCAA Tournament against St. Lawrence. Agosta scored the winning goal as the Lakers advanced for the first time. Then she scored another game-winner in the next round against Minnesota. The Lakers' run finally ended against Wisconsin in the national title game.

The consistent Agosta scored between 38 and 41 goals in all four of her college seasons. By the time she graduated in 2011, she had set an NCAA record with 157 career goals. Her 39 game-winning goals and 55 power-play goals were NCAA highs as well. Agosta was also dangerous shorthanded. She broke Krissy Wendell's mark of 16 career shorthanded goals by scoring 20.

Meghan Agosta, *in green*, scored 41 goals in 2008–09.

Hilary Knight had 38 assists in 2008–09.

HILARY KNIGHT

Before college, Hilary Knight competed in the 2006 Olympic Games. That's where she first met Wisconsin coach Mark Johnson, who was coaching Team USA. Johnson convinced the New Hampshire native to head west for college. In the fall of 2007, Knight arrived in Madison, Wisconsin.

The hard-shooting freshman scored 20 times on the way to an appearance in the 2008 national championship. Wisconsin lost that contest to Minnesota-Duluth. But Knight trained hard in the offseason. She improved her speed, stamina, and shooting.

The work paid off in 2008–09. Knight led the nation with 45 goals. That set a Wisconsin record. Knight also set school records by recording 83 points and netting 16 power-play goals during the season. Wisconsin rolled through the NCAA Tournament. Knight capped off the year by scoring three times and adding three assists in two Frozen Four games as Wisconsin captured its third national title.

After taking a season off to compete in the 2010 Olympics in Vancouver, Canada, Knight broke her own record by scoring 47 goals in 2010–11. In that season's NCAA Tournament, defenses keyed in on Knight. But she responded by relying on her playmaking. Knight had two assists in a 3–2 semifinal win over Boston College. She added another as Wisconsin went on to trounce Boston University 4–1 in the final.

Knight piled up 143 career goals. That was more than any men's or women's player in Wisconsin history. The old record holder was Mark Johnson. He cheered from the bench as Knight passed him in 2012.

AMANDA KESSEL

Amanda Kessel entered the 2013 NCAA semifinals with 97 points on the season. However, the Minnesota forward didn't score all game. The Golden Gophers edged out Boston College 3–2 in overtime. But they would need their junior star back on the scoreboard to finish the season a perfect 41–0.

Kessel delivered when Minnesota took on Boston University in the title game. Late in the first period, she fed teammate Hannah Brandt for a shorthanded goal. The score gave Minnesota a 2–0 lead. Early in the second, Kessel scored a goal of her own to put Minnesota up 3–1. The junior added a second assist early in the third period. Then she rounded off the 6–3 win by scoring an empty-net goal with 49 seconds left in the game. With her four-point performance, Kessel became just the fourth player in women's college hockey history to top 100 points in a season.

Kessel ended that season 74 points shy of the NCAA career scoring record. Then she left Minnesota to train with Team USA. Kessel suffered a concussion leading up to the 2014 Olympics. She played through the injury at first. But lingering symptoms kept her out of NCAA competition for two seasons. It seemed as if Kessel's career might be coming to an early end. She even retired for a brief time.

Kessel slowly recovered though. By early 2016, she was ready to play. She rejoined the Gophers for their final 13 games and helped the team get back to the Frozen Four. She then scored a game-tying goal on the way to a 3–2 win over Wisconsin in the semifinals. Kessel capped off her triumphant return by scoring the game-winner in a 3–1 championship win over Boston College.

Forward Amanda Kessel was named to the Frozen Four All-Tournament Team in 2015–16.

KENDALL COYNE

In February 2018, Kendall Coyne took the ice at the NHL's All-Star Skills competition. Facing off against some of the fastest men in the professional game, Coyne circled the ice in a blazing 14.226 seconds. Her time beat that of three NHL competitors. Only Connor McDavid made the loop faster, by less than a second.

Forward Kendall Coyne finished her career with a Northeastern-record 249 points.

Northeastern Huskies fans weren't surprised. Between 2011 and 2016, they had watched the 5-foot-2 forward rocket across the ice as she lifted the team to new heights. Coyne joined a Huskies team that had never been to the NCAA Tournament. Northeastern played in the shadow of local rivals Boston College and Boston University. Coyne immediately raised the bar. She posted 45 points as a freshman and guided the team to the city's coveted Beanpot title for the first time in more than 10 years.

In 2012–13, Coyne led the Huskies to another Beanpot title. She took the following season off to help Team USA win a silver medal at the 2014 Olympics in Sochi, Russia. Coyne returned to Northeastern in 2014–15. The next year, the senior carried Northeastern to its first-ever NCAA Tournament.

In the opening round, the Huskies faced No. 1 Boston College. Coyne scored Northeastern's only goal in a 5–1 loss. The score didn't impact the result, but it was still a huge milestone. Not only was it Northeastern's first tournament goal, it also marked Coyne's 50th goal of the season. She became only the second women's player to reach that mark. Coyne finished the year with a total of 84 points and won the Patty Kazmaier Award.

FAST FACT

Harvard's Nicole Corriero was the first women's player to pass 50 goals in a season. Corriero scored 59 over 36 games for the Crimson in 2004–05. She finished her career with 150 goals in 136 games.

JOHNNY GAUDREAU

With just over three minutes remaining in the 2012 NCAA men's championship game, Boston College led Ferris State 2–1. Eagles freshman Johnny Gaudreau picked up a bouncing puck at center ice. He kicked it from his skate to his stick as he entered the zone. Surrounded by two defenders, Gaudreau smoothly shifted from right to left, then back to the right. As the last Ferris State defender lunged to poke the puck away, Gaudreau lifted a backhand shot over the goalie's shoulder.

Gaudreau's play became known as "The Goal" to Boston College fans. The winger celebrated in his typical style. He veered away from the net and leapt into the glass before his teammates surrounded him. The Eagles were on their way to a national title, and their energetic freshman was a big reason for it.

At 5-foot-9, Gaudreau was undersized. But he made up for it with speed, incredible hands, and shifty skating. He also played the game with enthusiasm and passion. Gaudreau tallied 44 points as a freshman. Boston College fans began calling him "Johnny Hockey." The nickname stuck with Gaudreau for the rest of his career.

The Eagles didn't win another title after Gaudreau's first year. But he added to his legendary status with an incredible junior season in 2013–14. Gaudreau scored at least one point in 31 straight games. The last Hockey East player with a streak that long was Paul Kariya in 1992–93. Gaudreau finished the year with 36 goals and 44 assists. That made him only the second men's player since 2000 to collect 80 points in a season. The junior picked up the Hobey Baker Award before leaving school to begin an All-Star NHL career.

Winger Johnny Gaudreau, *right*, scored 80 points for Boston College in 2013–14.

CALE MAKAR

Cale Makar arrived in Amherst, Massachusetts, in the fall of 2017. It wasn't long before some fans began to wonder how long he would stay on campus. The Massachusetts (UMass) hockey team had never been strong. And Makar had just been drafted No. 4 overall

Massachusetts defenseman Cale Makar posted 49 points in 2018–19.

by the Colorado Avalanche. Many observers thought the slick-skating defenseman was ready for the NHL.

Makar stuck with UMass though. The freshman posted five goals and 16 assists and wowed his coaches with his ability to control the game from the blue line. However, UMass finished the season with more losses than wins. The hockey world once again predicted the talented defenseman would leave.

But once again, Makar stayed loyal to UMass. His leadership skills earned him a co-captain spot. And his 49 points that season fueled a huge turnaround for the Minutemen. UMass improved from 17 wins to 31 and reached the NCAA Tournament for just the second time in school history.

Introducing himself to the national audience, Makar posted an assist in a 4–0 opening-round win over Harvard. On defense, he helped hold the Crimson to just 17 shots. In the next round, Notre Dame mustered only 13 shots in another 4–0 UMass shutout. Makar scored his first goal of the tournament on a slap shot blast in the second period.

In the Frozen Four semifinals, Makar added an assist in a 4–3 overtime win over Denver. A day before the national championship game, he won the Hobey Baker Award. The Minutemen ended up losing to Minnesota-Duluth 3–0. But the sophomore defenseman had shown his skills. Within days of the loss, Makar was on the ice for the Avalanche in the Stanley Cup playoffs.

ÉLIZABETH GIGUÈRE

Élizabeth Giguère joined defending national champion Clarkson University in 2017. The Canadian forward managed to make the already-strong Golden Knights even better. She amassed 71 points in 41 games. That set a record for Clarkson freshmen.

Giguère also demonstrated a knack for clutch goals. In the 2018 NCAA Tournament, Clarkson and Mercyhurst went into overtime. Giguère's goal 16:52 into the extra session clinched a 2–1 win and a spot in the Frozen Four. In the semifinals, the Golden Knights again went into overtime. And Giguère again came through with a clutch play. She guided a pass to forward Loren Gabel, who beat the Ohio State goalie for the winner 16:12 into overtime. Clarkson won 1–0.

Only Colgate stood in the way of Clarkson's third NCAA title. Yet again, the game went to overtime. Just under eight minutes into the extra period, Giguère stole the puck at the Raiders' blue line. She stumbled while skating around a fallen defender. After recovering on one knee, she deked the goalie and slapped in a title-winning backhand.

Over the next three seasons, Giguère's quick thinking and even quicker hands led to 162 more points. The COVID-19 pandemic put an early end to the 2019–20 season. As a result, players were given an extra year of eligibility. Giguère transferred to Minnesota-Duluth to use hers. The fifth-year star put up 62 points in 40 games in 2021–22. Her college career ended in the national title game. This time, she scored a goal in a tight 3–2 loss to Ohio State. Giguère finished her career as the third-leading scorer in NCAA history with 294 points in 177 games.

Élizabeth Giguère celebrates after winning the national championship in 2018.

SOPHIE JAQUES

Defender Sophie Jaques arrived on Ohio State's campus in 2018. The Buckeyes hadn't won the WCHA tournament championship since 2001. And they had only been to the NCAA Tournament once.

Sophie Jaques recorded 59 points with Ohio State in 2021–22.

Jaques helped turn a disappointing team into champions. Buckeyes coach Nadine Muzerall marveled at the way the 5-foot-8 Jaques controlled the entire rink. In 2020, Jaques blocked three shots as Ohio State beat Wisconsin 1–0 in overtime to win the conference tournament. Days later, the COVID-19 pandemic shut down the season. When the sport came back in 2020–21, Jaques helped guide the team to the Frozen Four.

By 2021–22, Jaques was an offensive force as well as a defensive standout. In the WCHA title game, she scored two goals. The second was the overtime winner as the Buckeyes beat Minnesota 3–2. Jaques led the team with 59 points and was named a finalist for the Patty Kazmaier Award. Ohio State finished the season by capturing its first national title with a 3–2 win over Minnesota-Duluth.

Defenders rarely win the Kazmaier. By 2022–23, it hadn't happened for nearly two decades. Jaques ended the streak in style. She scored a team-high 24 goals and added 24 assists in 41 games on the way to earning the award.

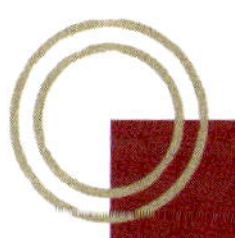

FAST FACT

Harvard's Angela Ruggiero was the first defensive player to win the Patty Kazmaier Award. She took home the honor after the 2003–04 season. Ruggiero finished the year with 20 goals and 30 assists.

HONORABLE MENTIONS

JOHN MAYASICH

A 6-foot-1, 216-pound forward, Mayasich posted 144 goals and 154 assists for Minnesota from 1951 to 1955. More than seven decades after he left college, no Golden Gopher had topped his scoring marks.

JOHN CULLEN

In the storied history of Boston University, no player has scored more points than Cullen. The 5-foot-10 forward put up 241 in a program-record 160 games. Cullen's finest season was in 1985–86. He put up 25 goals and 49 assists for the Terriers.

JIM MONTGOMERY

From 1989 to 1993, Montgomery posted 301 career points for Maine. The forward's three goals in the third period of the 1993 national championship are what fans remember most.

JULIE CHU

A master of the assist, Chu set an NCAA record with 197 helpers from 2003 to 2007. The 5-foot-8 Harvard forward won the Patty Kazmaier Award as a senior.

CONNOR HELLEBUYCK

Hellebuyck burst onto the college scene with a record .952 save percentage in his freshman season at UMass-Lowell. He recorded 12 shutouts and guided the underdog River Hawks to the 2012 Frozen Four.

JACK EICHEL

Eichel spent only one season at Boston University. In that time, the center racked up 26 goals and 45 assists while carrying the Terriers to the 2015 national championship. He became the first freshman since Paul Kariya in 1993 to win the Hobey Baker Award.

ANNE-RENÉE DESBIENS

From 2013 to 2017, Desbiens allowed only 109 goals in 122 games with Wisconsin. The goalie posted 21 shutouts in 2015–16. A year later, she won the Patty Kazmaier Award.

GLOSSARY

assist

A pass or shot that sets up a teammate to score a goal.

captain

The team leader and the only player allowed to speak to game officials regarding the rules.

conference

A group of schools that join together to create a league for their sports teams.

deke

A quick movement used to fake out an opponent.

hat trick

Three goals by the same player in one game.

lore

Well-known facts or stories.

overtime

An extra period of play when the score is tied after regulation.

retired

Ended one's career.

rival

An opponent with whom a player or team has a fierce and ongoing competition.

shorthanded

Playing with one fewer skater due to a penalty.

varsity

A school's top team in a sport.

MORE INFORMATION

BOOKS

Caraccioli, Tom, and Jerry Caraccioli. *Ice Breakers: A Kids' Guide to Hockey and the Greatest Players Who Changed the Game.* Quarto, 2025.

Clarke, David J. *Hockey Strategies*. Abdo, 2024.

Hewson, Anthony K. *GOATs of Hockey*. Abdo, 2022.

ONLINE RESOURCES

To learn more about the GOATs of college hockey, please visit **abdobooklinks.com** or scan this QR code. These links are routinely monitored and updated to provide the most current information available.

INDEX

ABOUT THE AUTHOR

Charlie Beattie is a writer, editor, and former sportscaster. Originally from Saint Paul, Minnesota, he now lives in Charleston, South Carolina, with his wife and son.